Ethics for the Information Age: Cases

Ethics for the Information Age: Cases

Effy Oz
Wayne State University

B&E TECH Business and Educational Technologies

Business and Educational Technologies
A Division of Wm. C. Brown Communications, Inc.

Vice President and Publisher *Susan A. Simon*
Acquisitions Editor *Paul Ducham*
Managing Developmental Editor *Linda Meehan Avenarius*
Advertising/Marketing Coordinator *Jennifer Wherry*
Product Development Assistant *Sandy Ludovissy*

 Wm. C. Brown Communications, Inc.

Chief Executive Officer *G. Franklin Lewis*
Corporate Senior Vice President and Chief Financial Officer *Robert Chesterman*
Corporate Senior Vice President and President of Manufacturing *Roger Meyer*
Executive Vice President/General Manager, Brown & Benchmark Publishers *Tom Doran*
Executive Vice President/General Manager, Wm. C. Brown Publishers *Beverly Kolz*

CONTENTS

FOREWORD

Information technology revolutionized the way in which we conduct many aspects of our lives. The tremendous technological advancement in the area of computers and related devices created unforeseen situations that necessitate new ethical consideration. Important issues like privacy, free speech, and protection of intellectual property have new meanings in the information age. The ease with which commercial values are transferred from one party to another with the help of computers and computer networks created new crimes. Ethics have to be modified to accommodate the vast changes brought upon us by the new technology.

Experience shows that the most effective method to teach ethics is to provoke the student with realistic cases. When discussing a case, the student should not be allowed to be a spectator. A case study puts the student in a dilemma that he or she alone has to solve. This book provides sixteen such provocative situations. The first case illustrates the difference between a relativist's and universalist's approach. The other cases depict situations that call for ethical judgment with respect to the proper use of information systems.

As in many ethical dilemmas, there is no right or wrong solution to each problem. My own guideline to my students is to judge each case along the utilitarian theory of "the greatest net good for the greatest number of people" or Kant's categorical imperative. However, it is often difficult to apply these theories to real-life scenarios. The purpose of case-based debates is to provoke the students' ethical thought and to try to synthesize solutions acceptable to the entire class. This will equip them with the appropriate knowledge to participate in the public debate on the above issues.

It is recommended that the students grapple with these cases after they read the appropriate chapter in a computer ethics book. I wish you lively and fruitful debates!

My appreciation to the following reviewers for their helpful comments:
R. Waldo Roth, Taylor University
Julian E. Boggess, Mississippi State University
Robert A. Barrett, Indiana–Purdue Fort Wayne

—E.O.

Luddonia and Summonia

Luddonia and Summonia are two small countries that share an island in the Pacific Ocean. The geographic situation is similar to that of Haiti and the Dominican Republic, which share an island in the Carribean sea. Any tourist could immediately see that the cultures of the two nations are significantly different. Luddonia is a democracy. Its citizens consider themselves among the most civilized people in the world. They value education and the arts. They are a peace-loving nation.

Summonia is ruled by a dictator, Colonel Sadam Papadoc, who seized control three years ago. A long series of dictators preceded him. Papadoc rules with an iron fist. He does not hesitate to charge with treason every citizen who opposes his regime. Of course the courts turn out verdicts that "the leader" expects. Many dissidents have been put in prison for long periods of time. Others have been executed. The Summonians are jealous of the Luddonians. Most of them hate the Luddonians with all their hearts. They believe that the entire island belongs to them. They trace this claim to an ancient tradition that is a part of their religion.

The Summonians are an aggressive people. Every few years they wage war against their neighbors. So far they have not managed to take even one square inch of land from the Luddonians, as the Luddonians maintain a small but highly trained and well-equipped military force. The last war took place two years ago. Since Summonia realized it could not beat its neighbor on the battle-field, it started sending commandos to disrupt life in Luddonia.

Summonian commandos kidnap Luddonian citizens, torture them, and lock them in jails for long periods. Some have been executed. Border villages are savagely attacked. Luddonia has retaliated with raids. Luddonian soldiers are instructed not to hurt innocent civilians. They are ordered to capture terrorists, either in uniform or not, and bring them to Luddonian territory for trial. Their task is frustrating, because their raids cannot stop the Summonian terrorists. The terror goes on, and Luddonian citizens have increasingly demanded that the government order the soldiers to use the enemy's methods. All the members of the Luddonian cabinet are sure that using such methods would put an end, or at least significantly minimize the attacks. But only two of the eleven members consistently demand such actions.

Luddonia's president, Mr. Kind, has repeatedly thwarted these demands. Capital punishment was abolished many years ago, and Parliament has time and again voted down bills to reinstate it. When terrorists are caught they receive a fair day in court. Many citizens claim that the only way to deter the Summonians is by using their own savage methods against them. Others argue that by using the same savage methods, Luddonia would lose its place among the free, civilized nations, and lower itself to the moral level of the Summonians.

DISCUSSION QUESTION

You are a citizen of Luddonia. What is your opinion: Should Luddonia react with the same methods that Summonia uses?

Data Alteration

Albert Koholik is a professional programmer. He works for $oftware, Inc., a small consulting firm that specializes in the development and maintenance of financial software. It sells services to banks, insurance companies, and brokerage houses. As most consulting firms refuse to assume maintenance assignments, $oftware has rendered a much-needed service to companies whose software was developed by others.

The strategy of offering maintenance service has proven highly profitable. When a client bank suddenly loses customer records, it calls $oftware to solve the problem. In many such cases $oftware's experts find that the records are still there, but could not be accessed. They work many hours until they debug the program. Occasionally, clients need modifications to programs to accommodate new business needs.

Often, $oftware's professionals have to work over weekends, when the client company does not serve customers. They usually stay alone in the company's facility, working round the clock until the problem is solved or the required modification completed. As part of its contract, $oftware has a clause that guarantees the absolute observance of confidentiality. Also, every person hired by $oftware signs a pledge not to divulge any confidential information that he or she may come across in the course of his or her professional work.

Al has built himself a reputation as a knowledgeable, conscientious professional. He has mastered various programming languages, including COBOL, FORTRAN, RPG, C, and FOCUS. But his most important asset is the expertise he has acquired as a debugger of complex program modules. Since he is single, he does not mind working on weekends. The pay is good, and "now is the time to make money for a later time, when I marry and have a family," he says.

Last May, Al was assigned to modify a credit approval program for a bank. He was asked to install the programmed module on Sunday, when no one was in the facility except for a security guard. He finished the assignment earlier than he envisioned. While he was taking a last look at the program, he was intrigued by one of the items on the main menu. This option allowed the user to connect to the information system of EquiCredit Co. EquiCredit is a company that sells credit histories of individuals and organizations. The bank routinely taps this information pool for data on clients who ask for loans. The bank pays EquiCredit an annual flat fee for the service.

Although there are other companies that provide this service, there was some chance that this company had information concerning his credit history. After all, he held three different credit cards. It took him a few seconds to find out how to navigate in the large database. Lo and behold, his own record was there. He moved his head closer to the computer monitor and read the information. All of a sudden his face blushed. "What the hell is that? Idiots!"

The record said he was late on a monthly payment of a student loan. Indeed, seven years earlier he had taken out a loan for his college studies, but he never made a late payment in his life. What should he do? On the one hand, there was probably no real risk in this note. He had received his credit cards without any problem. On the other hand, there could be an explanation for that. Maybe the erroneous note got in the file *after* he received the credit cards. Also, the note might not be of concern to the issuers of *these* cards, but may hamper his quest for a loan in the future.

Al knew it was difficult to have a credit information company correct records. He had also read of cases like this in which people were denied credit without any apparent reason. He decided not to be the victim of wrong information. He figured out a way to circumvent the security module of EquiCredit, and erased the note.

On Monday, Al's boss congratulated him for another successful completion of a task. The bank was satisfied with the modification to its program.

DISCUSSION QUESTIONS

1. Was Al's act unethical? Why? Base your answer on *deontological* and *utilitarian* ethical theories.
2. You are Al. (1) Would you peek into the credit database? (2) If you peeked, what would you do (change the data, notify EquiCredit, or what)?

Worker Displacement

"This system is going to save our client twenty-two salaries. Once their competitors hear about it, we're going to be swamped with work."

"Yep. It's been really a good experience."

It is a sunny afternoon. You sit with Randy under a parasol, sipping fruit cocktail from large glasses. You received this short vacation as a token of gratitude from the company you both work for, which specializes in automotive robots. Until recently, inspection of assembled parts was done manually, but you have designed a system that controls robots who replace human inspectors. Clearly, your contribution took computerization one step ahead in the automotive industry.

Randy, your friend and coworker, puts the glass on the table and stares at the ocean's rolling waves. His smile turns into a pensive expression.

"What's wrong, Randy?" you ask.

"Well, my uncle once worked for an automaker. He was an expert car painter but after twenty-six years he got the pink slip. 'Thank you for your loyal service' or something like that."

"I don't see the point," you say.

"The point is very simple. He was replaced by a robot. Some wise guy like us sold the company a computer-based robot that did the job as effectively as my uncle did for a fraction of the cost."

Randy picks up the glass and sips slowly. He doesn't look at you; instead his eyes follow the beautiful waves breaking on the white sand. Then he goes on.

"Can you imagine? He worked there since he had been out of the service at the age of twenty-one. A forty-seven-year-old man who loved his job was thrown out of work."

"Did he find another job?" you ask.

"No. How could he? Car painting was his expertise. He was very good at it and used to get a monthly bonus for doing cars above the required norm. He asked to be retrained. The company didn't offer any retraining. After that he collected unemployment, then worked a little here, a little there. He barely made ends meet. Sad. Very sad. He was too old to start a new career, if you can call car painting a career, and too young to retire."

You are silent. You see the connection between your professional feat and Randy's story. He goes on.

"Here it goes again. Our beautiful computer system is terminating people. People who feed families and try to send their kids to college."

He has a point, you think. It has crossed your own mind several times. But you are convinced that you are doing the right thing. You want to calm him down and quiet his compunctions.

"Randy, I know what you're feeling, but I think you're taking this too personally. You have to consider the bigger picture. The systems that you and I and the other guys back at RoboSoft are developing help society to advance."

Randy turns his face to you.

"Is laying off twenty-two people 'advancement'?"

"Well, *we* didn't lay them off. The company will. Of course we are helping the company, but if we didn't, someone else would. The world is moving forward."

Randy shakes his head. You try another approach.

"Look. Two thousand years ago almost all members of society were busy growing food. This didn't change until the industrial revolution. After the industrial revolution, fewer and fewer people worked in the fields because agricultural machines did most of the dirty work. Do you know how many Americans now work in agriculture? Three percent! What is happening now in manufacturing is similar to this. Fewer and fewer people work in manufacturing, because machines can do their jobs for a fraction of the cost. We help this to happen."

"But millions lose their jobs!" Randy says.

"That may be," you say, "but you enjoy the benefits of this."

"I enjoy the benefits? What benefits?"

"Goods made with the aid of computers are less expensive. Yes, the manufacturer may make a greater profit, but you enjoy a cheaper product. Your standard of living goes up. Less expensive production spurs the economy. Don't we all enjoy the results?"

"Well, I would be careful with the words 'we all'. My uncle didn't enjoy being laid off. He is still struggling. And as to societal benefits: one more jobless person is one less taxpayer. Who do you think pays my uncle his unemployment money? You and I, with our taxes. And all those people who lose their jobs now spend less. They can't afford to buy many of the 'cheaper' products."

Yes, he has a point.

"What do you suggest should be done, Randy?"

"I would expect the government to provide retraining courses for laid-off people. Or, maybe, force employers to retrain their workers."

"I'm not sure the latter proposition is good. In many industries, especially in manufacturing, entire jobs become obsolete." You try to be tactful, but feel compelled to hit the nail on the head. "Take your uncle's old job, for example. His employer probably doesn't need more than one worker per assembly line to monitor a robot painter. What could the company retrain your uncle to do?"

"I guess you are right."

"And don't forget our obligation to the profession. It is our duty to further the benefits the economy can draw from computer-based systems. When we succeed, we make companies aware of our expertise, and create jobs for young computer professionals."

"Yes. Yes. I guess you're right."

Randy and you lean back in your chairs, and stare at the far horizon. There's only one day left to enjoy this calm atmosphere. Then it's off to your desks in Chicago and back to the new project your boss has assigned.

DISCUSSION QUESTIONS

1. On the plane back to Chicago you think about Randy's concerns. Yes, you made several good points, but he had a good point too. What do you suggest government should do for workers displaced by computers?
2. What can employers do to minimize worker displacement by computers?

Monitoring E-mail

Barbara Baranek is a senior partner at a Big Six accounting firm. She runs the Detroit branch. The firm is completely computerized; there is a personal computer on almost every desk, including the desks of the secretaries. Many of the accountants have word processors and spreadsheet programs installed locally on their own computers.

A year ago, a consulting company installed a local area network (LAN) in the office. A PC with a large storage capacity is used as the file-server. The network allows everybody to share programs and data. One of the great features it provides is electronic mail (E-mail). Since the offices are housed on three floors, workers who wanted to talk to their peers had to use their phones. If the person they wanted was not available, they had to either leave a message with a secretary or call again later. Much time was lost. Now, with the LAN, all they have to do is use the computer to type up a message and launch it. Employees are required to check their E-mail frequently. This way everyone is assured that the message was received.

The employees like the E-mail so much that they have started to communicate this way even when neither party is away. Because the LAN is connected through a bridge to branches in other cities, everyone who has access to a computer (and that includes virtually all the office workers) could send messages to and receive messages from the other branches. Of course, communications time costs money.

As manager of the branch, Barbara could peek into the electronic mailboxes of the employees, but she had never done this until last Tuesday. She was sitting in her comfortable swivel chair eating a sandwich when she pulled the LAN's user manual from her bottom drawer and looked for the chapter that explained how to override passwords to other users' E-mail boxes. It was as easy as 1-2-3. She logged onto the box of Brandon Schneider, an accounting graduate of Wayne State University who was in his first year of practice toward becoming a CPA.

Yep! There was a message waiting for Brandon. But it had nothing to do with accounting. It read:

From: Contelli

To: Schneider

05–06–1992 09:32

Per your E-mail message:

No, I don't have plans for tomorrow night. I guess you are the new would-be CPA. No problem. Dinner would be fine. I think you should know that I'm vegetarian, though. Let me know what time.

—Lisa

Barbara was not amused. The firm's policy strictly forbade employees to use the system for personal correspondence. She immediately sent her own message to Brandon, instructing the young man to report to her office, where she admonished him for his behavior. Brandon claimed he had not been aware of the policy. Barbara did not accept that as justification. She told Brandon that he would not receive the promised bonus, and that if the incident was repeated, he would be fired.

DISCUSSION QUESTIONS

1. Do you accept Barbara's peeking into Brandon's E-mail box?
2. Was Brandon's behavior unethical?
3. Suppose Brandon knew the firm's policy. Would you change your answer to question 2?

Conflicts and Priorities

Lars Lawson is a senior systems analyst at PowerSoft, Inc. PowerSoft is a consulting firm that specializes in computer programs for power stations. The company employs two engineers whose formal training and experience are in nuclear power. However, their knowledge is not sufficient for actually designing any facilities. The engineers work as senior programmers. Their formal training allows them to better understand the technical environment in which they operate.

Specifically, PowerSoft specializes in programs that control radiation. The company installs a microcomputer, or a series of microcomputers, in the power plant and writes programs that alert against radiation above the safe level. The firm installs a turn-key system, i.e., a system that is ready for operation without any need for preparation on the client's part. To build the alert system, Power-Soft receives specifications from the client. The specifications include locations for radiation sensors, safety levels of radiation, details of existing computers to which the sensors can be hooked up, and other technical details.

Few consultants specialize in this field. PowerSoft, therefore, became a nationally recognized authority within just three years of its establishment. The firm built systems and provided related consulting services to more than thirty power plants in the U.S. A year ago it started to offer its services to foreign governments; it was now working on a large project in Sweden.

PowerSoft is highly profitable. One reason, of course, is the small competition. Another is the fact that many nuclear plants are built according to identical, or similar, plans. When a client signs a contract for a new plant, PowerSoft's sales engineer first checks to see if the plant is similar in floor layout and operations to that of one or more other clients that the firm has already served. If it is, the systems analysts apply the same software to the new site. Sometimes just a few modifications are needed. The firm's profit in a case like this is huge, because the bulk of the work, the systems design and programming, is already done. All that is needed is installation.

Lars was now involved in a project in southern California. Installation of the system was completed two days ago. The first test was fine; no problems were detected. The most important test consisted of a simulation of overradiation and radiation leaks. The sensors are laid out in bands. The first band is installed very close to the core, the second one, in a greater radius, and the third is installed outside, around the plant. The radiation leaks that the sensors are designed to detect are smaller as the radius grows. That is, the external band is programmed to trigger the alarm for a significantly smaller amount of radiation than the one closest to the core.

While testing, it occurred to Lars that the external band was not identical to the plan he and his peers used. When PowerSoft received the plant's specifications, they looked identical to those of the plant that PowerSoft worked on a year ago in Montana. The same company that built the nuclear plant there built this one. And the company that owns and operates the California plant also owns and operates the Montana plant. So there was no reason to suspect that the specifications would be different. Indeed, when PowerSoft's engineers reviewed the specifications given to them before the contract was signed, they looked exactly the same as those of the Montana plant.

Lars figured there was a very remote chance that all three bands would malfunction at the same time. However, he felt that he should alert his supervisor, James Nord. Nord was the firm's chief systems analyst and a partner. With two other computer professionals, he left a company that built nuclear reactors to establish PowerSoft. Both clients and employees revered him as a capable professional, good manager, and honest businessman.

Lars called the office in Pennsylvania and asked to talk to James. James listened carefully. He then said: "Leave the system as is."

Lars was surprised. "I'm sorry, can you repeat that?"

"Leave the system as is."

"Sir, I'm not sure you understand. We implemented a program that does not completely fit the specifications. It—"

"No, Lars, it does fit the specifications. The specifications may not exactly fit the real layout, but that is not our problem. What is the probability of total failure?"

"I can't tell exactly. I guess about 1:100,000."

Although a 1:100,000 chance that the system would fail to correspond to all sensors at the same time was not great, it was twice the standard promised to PowerSoft's clients. James's voice was calm.

"That's good enough."

"But why not let them know they made a mistake in the specifications? We can charge them for the modifications."

"Lars, listen to me. I know this company. I know the people who run it. They will not admit their failure. Once they know, they'll expect us to modify free of charge. Even if they admitted their failure, we simply don't have the time. We have two other contracts, and we have to be out of there by next week."

Lars was upset. The few seconds of silence seemed like an hour. James sensed what was going on in his employee's head. His voice now turned low but stern.

"Lars, not a word to the client. You did your job to my full satisfaction. The project is *my* responsibility. You have nothing to worry about. I'll see you here in two days."

"Well, OK. Yes, I'll see you on Thursday."

They hung up. On the plane, on his way back to Pennsylvania, Lars thought over and over about his conversation with James. He wasn't sure what was the right thing to do.

DISCUSSION QUESTIONS

1. Do you accept that James is fully responsible for the system, and therefore Lars should take no further action?
2. Lars has a dilemma of obligations. As a professional he has to choose among obligations to several parties. Who are the parties?
3. If you were in Lars's place, what would you do?

Obligations to Clients

Maria Delgado joined Business Systems, Inc. (BSI), two years ago, right after she graduated from Hahvahd University. She majored in computer science, and hoped to start her own consulting business one day. BSI offered her a high salary and a good environment for accumulating experience. Since she had joined the firm two years ago she was assigned primarily to analyze and design inventory information systems for small businesses. She enjoyed her work.

A month ago BSI signed a contract with Shertz & Pantz, a small retailer of men's clothing. Shertz & Pantz started as a single store. Its prices are low. The owners, two young men named Jack Shertz and Lloyd Pantz, prepare their own leaflets, which they mail directly to households. Their main clientele is young men between the ages of 20 and 35. This has worked very well. A bank willingly loaned the owners money to open two new stores. Business is booming. The owners plan to open another three stores in the next two years.

Due to the fast growth, Jack contacted five systems consulting firms. He wanted to convert the manual inventory handling into a computer-based system. The system would track inventory in all the stores. This way he could keep track of the overall demand for specific items, but also learn which items sell better or worse in which stores. He was looking for a system that could grow with the business.

Since BSI had a good reputation and its price proposal was one next to the lowest, Shertz & Pantz selected it to build the system. The contract was for a turn-key system. That meant BSI would purchase the hardware, develop the software, install the system, and ascertain it could be operated immediately.

Four BSI professionals were developing the system. Maria was second in command to Gilbert Ross, a veteran computer professional. Gilbert was known as a good project manager. He always emphasized meeting deadlines. He never missed a deadline in his entire fifteen year-career; perhaps this was why he was known as "the slave driver" among the firm's employees. Whenever his team faced a technical problem, his people and he worked round the clock until the problem was resolved. This project had proceeded without a glitch. In fact, Gilbert expected to introduce the system two weeks before deadline.

Three weeks before delivery Maria started the final tests. She performed all the necessary mock transactions: adding a new item; sale of different quantities of a specific item; entering an order to a supplier; etc. All worked well, within reasonable time limits. She proceeded to test the customer transaction module to see how long a sales entry would take. To that end she entered 2,000 records and measured the time it took to then enter a transaction. The average time was within what she considered reasonable. She then doubled the number to 4,000 and added individual transactions at this point. The system's acknowledgement came after 10 seconds, which was too slow. She tried another transaction. Again, it took 10 seconds for the system to respond. Maria reduced the number of records to 3,000, and made a sales entry. The response took 8 seconds. "Still too slow," she muttered.

Gilbert gathered his team daily in his office to discuss progress. Maria asked to see the contract with Shertz & Pantz. "What do you need the contract for?" Gilbert asked. "I'm just curious about something," Maria answered.

Gilbert pulled the contract from his desk drawer and handed it to her. While the others were talking, Maria opened the document to the specifications sections. Much to her surprise she did not find any benchmarks.

Benchmarks are the limits of system operations that the client agrees to tolerate. For example, the client may require that a certain type of transaction does not take longer than a specified number of seconds.

"Gilbert, I—" Maria stopped. She realized she was interrupting one of her colleagues.

"That's OK. Go ahead." the colleague said.

"I'm afraid we have a little problem. I started to test the system yesterday. It is slow."

"Slow?" Gilbert said, "What do you mean slow? How slow?"

Maria told them what happened when she increased the number of records. Gilbert did not look disturbed.

"What was the average time with 1,000 records?"

"A second to a second and a half."

"And with 2,000 records?"

"A second and a half to two seconds."

"Then what's the problem?" Gilbert asked. "They only have about 1,000 sales per day."

"Well," Maria said quietly, "As far as I remember, Jack Shertz said they expected to open additional stores, and since we are connecting all of them into the same database, the daily transactions will increase."

Gilbert sighed and leaned back.

"Look, Maria, we have a contract with Shertz & Pantz. We are providing them with a good information system that meets their business requirements. We cannot be responsible for future developments in our clients' businesses."

These words did not convince Maria, but she was reluctant to antagonize her boss. She moved uneasily in her chair. Her colleagues looked at her, but apparently they had decided not to intervene. Gilbert felt Maria was disturbed. He leaned forward.

"Maria, we have a contract with them. They signed it. We signed it. They knew what they were getting for their money—"

"But that's the point," Maria interrupted him. "I'm not sure they knew what they were getting for their money. A year from now they will discover the system is too slow for them."

"Do you think the problem is in the hardware or in the software?" Gilbert asked.

"Come on, Gilbert. Give me some credit. Of course the problem is not with the software."

"Then why didn't you voice your opinion when we decided on the GTX?"

The GTX was an IBM computer clone. BSI purchased it for turn-key systems directly from the manufacturer. It was considered a good machine for a low price. So far, BSI had installed them in small, one-site businesses.

"Because I'm not in charge of hardware, and I never encountered speed problems with this machine." Maria tried to keep a low tone.

"Maria, the machines were purchased, and we cannot return them without a penalty. As I said, we signed a fair and square contract with Shertz & Pantz. They will receive a good system two weeks before the deadline. Let's move on."

Maria kept silent through the rest of the meeting. She felt it was BSI's responsibility to assure that the systems it developed could serve the clients in the present as well as in the future. She was sure Gilbert was being unfair to the client. But she debated whether she, Maria, should do anything about it.

DISCUSSION QUESTIONS

1. Is anything wrong with Gilbert's behavior? If so, what is it that is wrong?

2. If you were in charge of the contract with Shertz & Pantz, would you write the contract differently? How and why?

3. Put yourself in Maria's shoes. What would you do now: continue work as usual or notify the client about future problems with the system (facing sure dismissal by BSI)? Put this project behind you, but voice your opinion in future deals with clients?

ETHICS CASE 7

High-tech Diagnosis

John Hart is a retired real estate agent. He retired from Century 22 a year ago, and had plans to spend his free time with his wife, two daughters, and five grandchildren. Over the years, he had accumulated a nice pension that would allow him to live the rest of his life in comfort. He planned to take his wife, Adrianne, on a tour of Europe, and perhaps later on a trip to Japan.

Two months ago John had a strange feeling in the bottom left part of his back. For a week he did not say anything to Adrianne, but when the strange feeling turned into a light pain, he told his wife. She suggested that he see a doctor. Like many men of his age he refused, saying "Ah, it's nothing. I'm sure it'll go away soon." When Adrianne entreated him, he reluctantly agreed. She took him to the doctor.

Dr. Seak was a new physician in the clinic. A few years ago he graduated from James Hopkeans University, whose medical school is known for its enthusiastic adoption of hightech instruments and modern methods. He greeted John and Adrianne warmly. John tried to dismiss the light pain in his back as "nothing," but Adrianne explained that he had never suffered from back pain. "He never complains unless it really bothers him," she said, "and I'm afraid this may be more serious than he thinks. I just want to be sure."

Dr. Seak agreed with her. He asked John to show him exactly where the pain was and what kind of pain it was, throbbing or continuous. He immediately sent John to have his back X-rayed. The photographs were in his hands fifteen minutes later and he examined them carefully. John and Adrianne felt he was not sure what to conclude from the photos. He then pointed to the computer on his desk and said:

"This little computer contains a new program called "Esclapius." It's an expert system. It contains medical expertise on back pains and treatments from one of the best experts in the world. I'm going to ask a few questions, enter the data, and receive a diagnosis and suggested treatment. Do you have any objections?"

"Well, no. Why should I?" John said. "I count on you."

The young doctor sat at the computer and pressed a few keys. A long series of questions appeared on the monitor. The physician read the questions to John, and when John answered, he keyed in the responses. He asked about previous illnesses, illnesses John's parents had, eating and drinking habits, the type of work John did, and many other questions. After he made the final entry, he sat back and waited.

"Now we'll see what the system thinks."

A few lines appeared on the screen, and Dr. Seak leaned forward to read the output. John noticed a change of expression in his face. The doctor read the lines twice or three times, and apparently was not happy. He turned in his swivel chair to face John and said:

"I'm afraid I don't have good news, Mr. Hart. Apparently, you have Khanylitis. It's a rare disease. I don't know how to tell you this. It's terminal."

John was petrified. Adrianne said, "Excuse me, doctor. Are you sure?"

"This comes from *the* expert in the area. I couldn't make a better judgment myself. Of course, if you want to, you can ask for a second opinion."

He explained the nature of the disease, how it progresses, and how the patient should change his or her life-style in order to postpone death. The Harts were shocked. Yes, they said, they certainly wanted a second opinion. Dr. Seak gave them a short list of expert doctors. Adrianne took the list, but after they left, the two decided that they would approach a physician who was not on the list. They wanted to consult with someone who did not even know Dr. Seak.

That next day they were sitting in Dr. Small's office. They had received his name from a friend who once had a friend who died from Khanylitis. Somehow she remembered the name of the doctor. A series of telephone calls to the local hospitals yielded the doctor's telephone number. Small had some experience with patients who suffered from the disease and John and Adrianne hoped he could give them a better diagnosis than Dr. Seak. Dr. Small agreed to see them so soon despite his busy schedule. He asked that they bring along the X rays. He took a long look at them.

"To be honest with you, I can't make a decisive judgment. I'll have to ask you a few questions," he said.

John answered Dr. Small's questions. The doctor quickly wrote down the answers on a yellow legal pad. After he finished, he told the couple he would call them within two days to tell them the diagnosis.

John and Adrianne jumped at every ring of the phone the next day. Finally, Dr. Small called with the bad news. The diagnosis was Khanylitis. He anticipated that John would live about six months, which was identical to Dr. Seak's prediction. Dr. Small suggested that John avoid any fatty foods, refrain from salt and alcoholic beverages, and try to rest as much as possible.

John and Adrianne were devastated. Of course, the trips to Europe and Japan were out of the question. It is so ironic, Adrianne thought, that now, when John should enjoy all the things he could not enjoy before he retired, he can hardly enjoy anything. John took reality more calmly than his wife. He was not a religious person, but had always accepted things as they came. If it happened, he said, then it probably had to happen. Their children started to visit more often. The daughters made sure that at least one of them, with her husband and the Harts' grandchildren, spent each weekend with John and Adrianne.

Five months went by. John told his wife that he didn't feel any change in his back. "Yes, it hurts from time to time, but no more than it did five months ago," he said. Adrianne was sure he was pretending. She expected his health to deteriorate, but it didn't. At the end of the sixth month Adrianne called Dr. Small and scheduled an appointment. When she and John showed up in the doctor's office, there was another man there, not wearing a white lab coat.

"Please meet Professor Gutek. He is an expert on back diseases, and has more experience with Khanylitis than any other doctor in America. He is visiting our hospital and I thought he could help solve the mystery we are facing in your case, Mr. Hart."

Professor Gutek asked that John have his back X-rayed again. He examined the X rays. Then he examined John's back with his hands. With every movement of his palms he asked John whether he felt any pain. Professor Gutek eventually spotted the source of the pain and he looked again at the X rays. He then asked John to dress and wait with Adrianne in the hallway. While they were sitting in the hallway, Professor Gutek left the room without saying a word to them. Soon, Dr. Small asked them in.

"I have excellent news," he said, but he did not smile. "You are going to live a long life. You have a benign tumor that is mildly pressing on your spine when you make certain movements. We can remove it if you want us to, or you can live with it if it doesn't bother you too much. In any case, you don't have Khanylitis."

"I, I don't understand. How . . . how could this happen? Two doctors give an opinion, and it turns out to be wrong. How . . . ?" John shook his head.

"Mr. Hart," Dr. Small said quietly. "Remember I asked you many questions? I entered your answers into a special computer program, an expert system. It helped me diagnose your case. Apparently, the computer diagnosis was wrong. I am terribly sorry."

Both John and Adrianne felt as if they were reborn. At home, after they told the good news to their children and friends, it dawned on them that both Dr. Seak and Dr. Small used the same computer program. Something must be wrong with that program. They lived six months waiting for death, not being able to leave their home, not being able to do the things they had been wanting to for so many years. And all because of some computer program.

Some of their friends suggested that they sue and seek compensation for their anguish. They didn't know whom to sue.

DISCUSSION QUESTIONS

1. Whose fault could the erroneous diagnosis be? Who is responsible to the patient for the erroneous diagnosis?
2. Should doctors (and other specialists whose opinions have significant impact on people's lives) be allowed to count on artificial intelligence for their decisions?

Obligations to Employer

Ameritel, Inc., was established as a consortium of three of the largest hotel companies and five car rental firms. The purpose of the consortium was to offer the public hotel and car rental services. The charge of the new organization would be simple: to administer a reservation information system. The idea was similar to that implemented in the air travel industry. One reservation system served many airlines. Travel agencies had terminals in their offices from which they could retrieve current and accurate information on flights: flight numbers, departure and arrival times, prices, etc.

Obviously, Ameritel executives wanted to hire the best consulting firm to develop the reservation system. The selection process took three months. Ameritel's president, Ken Horwitz, knew from his experience that it would be best to split work on the system into two major jobs: (1) development of requirements and a RFQ (request for quotation), and (2) the development of the system itself. He intended to assign the jobs to two separate companies to assure quality.

Henderson Consulting Co. was hired to develop the requirements and RFQ. Highly experienced people spent long hours with Ameritel management. After eight weeks, the requirements were ready. Henderson's people laid out the general architecture of the system, including hardware recommendations. The RFQ was now ready for bidding. With Ameritel's consent, the Henderson team named the system Reserv.

According to Ameritel's agreement with Henderson, the latter would participate in selecting the best company to develop Reserv. Horwitz did not want to leave the entire job to Henderson, because of the possibility that its team would reject competitors it did not like. He felt that as long as he and other executives from the consortium were on the selection committee, the selection process would be impartial. Of course, he reserved for himself the final say. Henderson sent the RFQ to 25 firms, the most experienced organizations in development of large business databases. The plan was to have two selection sessions. In the first meeting, the highest 21 proposals were culled out. In the second meeting, the committee considered both total price and technical details. Previous experience and time were a major factor. It was imperative to have Reserv in place within eighteen months. After a long deliberation, the committee chose Software of America, Inc. (SOA), to develop the system.

SOA allotted a team of 32 systems analysts and programmers for the $17 million project. Clifford Charles, one of the company's three vice presidents, headed the effort full time. He defined four modules and appointed an experienced systems analyst to lead each module subteam. He shortened the timetable proposed in the RFQ by six months to leave him enough slack in case something went wrong with the original plan of work. To assure adherence to the timetable, he met the subteam leaders daily, for thirty to sixty minutes. Clifford was known as a tough project manager who did not tolerate deviations from his plans.

The first three phases were accomplished on time. The final phase was to be the integration of the different modules, and the writing of the program's main menu and application. This is usually a difficult phase, because the modules may prove incompatible. Clifford expected the main application to be written within two weeks. This was a relatively small program that "tied" all the other programs into one application.

Clifford scheduled the beginning of the integration for the last week of the fourteenth month. He figured that would leave a month for testing the system at the SOA facility, and another month for installation and testing at the first two test sites, which were a Barriot hotel and a Mavis car rental office. Barriot and Mavis were major stakeholders in the Ameritel consortium. Clifford put himself at the lead of the integration effort and told his people he would even involve himself in programming, if his help was needed. He gave them the feeling he was not just "managing from above," but that he was involved in every bit of the system.

Two days after the integration, one of his subteam leaders called him and said something "snapped." Clifford checked the snag and worked with the subteam to debug it. Although two of the programmers said they suspected the problem would surface again in the future, he ordered them to continue the integration. According to the contract, two thirds of the total price was to be paid when Reserv was ready for testing on-site. Another sixth was to be paid after one month of running live data. The last sixth was due two months later, provided the system worked without a glitch. Clifford was determined to be paid on time.

Luci Maas, a young systems analyst, headed the car rental module. That was the module in which the problem had occurred. Apparently the module worked well before its integration into the "big picture," but something in the "seams" between the module and the main application was flawed. She suspected the problem stemmed from the use of SOA's CASE (computer aided software engineering) tool, which made the car rental database inflexible. Luci asked Clifford to give her more time to try to locate the problem and fix it.

"How much time do you need?" he asked.

"Two weeks."

"You've got it, but not an hour more."

She and her people worked round the clock. Indeed, she traced the problem to the CASE tool she used. However, she could not fix it. She called Clifford and told him of her finding.

"What are you telling me, Luci? You can't fix it?"

"I can, but we would have to redo much of the module."

"Because you'll have to use another CASE tool, right?"

"Right."

"That's out of the question. What's the worst case scenario when operating the system?"

Luci had a ready answer, but she hesitated. Clifford sounded impatient and although she used the same CASE tool that she and her colleagues had used for years, she knew Clifford would hold her responsible. But she felt it was her duty to tell him the truth.

"If Reserv crashes, it will be unrecoverable."

Clifford was livid.

"What are the chances that it will happen?"

"I really can't tell," Luci answered.

Clifford paused for a few seconds, and then said, "Forget it. We're moving ahead as scheduled."

Clifford realized that rectifying the car rental module meant a failure to meet he deadline. This would put a dent in SOA's reputation. It would also cause significant financial damage. Worse, according to the contract a delay of more than three months entitled Ameritel to assign the project, or what was left to be completed, to another contractor. Therefore, he did not say a word to his boss, SOA's president. He knew he was taking a huge risk. If anything went wrong with Reserv, he alone would have to absorb the hit.

A month later Reserv was tested in the two sites with live reservation data. A few weeks later, as scheduled, SOA's president officially delivered the system to Ken Horwitz in a highly publicized ceremony. The system was touted as the most advanced reservation system in the travel industry. As planned, Ameritel started efforts to market Reserv's services to other hotel and car rental chains.

DISCUSSION QUESTIONS

1. Clifford felt that he should not tell his boss about the system's problem out of loyalty to his boss. How would you act if you were in Clifford's shoes?
2. You are Luci. What would you do after your discussion with Clifford?

Miscommunications

Jeff Bordic was happy. The numbers his accountant just showed him were beyond his expectations for this quarter. Plastico, Inc., the enterprise he started three years ago, was doing extremely well. It produced biodegradable plastic products, especially disposable dishes. The products became very popular with young families who were environmentally conscientious. The dishes were artfully decorated and their popularity boosted sales fourfold in the three years of the company's existence.

Jeff's labor force doubled from 32 to 64 over the past year. Although the manufacturing and packing operations are highly automated, he felt that personnel would have to grow to deal with marketing, shipping, design of new products, and other disciplines. Even the current number of employees was too big to handle manually. His accountant suggested that he start thinking of a personnel information system for the company.

Jeff acknowledged the necessity. The accountant gave him the names of a few small consulting firms. She recommended the one that topped the list, SBIS (Small Business Information Systems). It was a partnership of five computer professionals who concentrated on purchasing, recommendation, and development of information systems. They specialized in personnel and payroll systems. Jeff contacted them and his call was transferred to Odessa Washington. Odessa met Jeff in Jeff's office.

The accountant and Jeff explained how they currently managed personnel. The accountant described how she collected time cards once a week, and calculated the gross pay, taxes, and net pay of the workers. Odessa nodded frequently. This was a typical small company, doing all this work manually. As with all these small companies that grew in a short period of time, the managers of this one, too, did not exactly know what a computer-based information system could do for them. They simply wanted a computer to do automatically much of what they had been doing manually.

There were a few characteristics of Plastico's remuneration that Odessa had not seen before. Compensation was a combined function of time and output. In a way, there was profit sharing at Plastico. Jeff wouldn't call it "profit sharing," but the bonuses he gave his workers were a fixed percentage of the company's profit. He told Odessa he wanted this feature in the system. This and other required features excluded the purchase of an off-the-shelf software package. That meant SBIS would have to develop the system from scratch. The advantage was that the system could be specifically tailored to Plastico's needs.

Plastico's accountant had one microcomputer on her desk. The secretaries of Jeff and the accountant shared another personal computer for word processing. Odessa recommended the purchase of a separate, high-speed, high-capacity microcomputer for the new system. She told Jeff that SBIS did not endorse any hardware and that the hardware purchase could be done directly by the client according to SBIS specifications. If the client wanted SBIS to purchase the hardware, they would find the best deal, but charge 5% for handling. Jeff asked that Odessa "purchase the best computer for us."

"You need a 486 micro with a math co-processor, four to five megabytes of RAM, and about 80 megabytes of storage. For your reports I recommend that we add a laser printer. We can also—" She stopped when she noticed Jeff and the accountant were smiling, somewhat embarrassed.

"Ms. Washington," Jeff said quietly, "all this doesn't mean much to us. We want you to decide what's best for us, purchase the right equipment, and include it in the deal."

"Okay, okay," Odessa smiled too. "We'll take care of it. No problem."

"Can you tell us how much the new system will cost?" Jeff asked.

"I have to take my notes to the office and put a few figures together. Can I call you sometime tomorrow afternoon?"

"Of course."

Odessa shook hands with Jeff and the accountant, and left. The following day she called Plastico. Jeff accepted the price, and a day later the contract was signed.

After they conceptualized the new information system and designed its components, SBIS often hired outside programmers to do the programming itself. The same thing occurred here. Odessa drew data flow diagrams of the new system and input and output screens, and designed, on paper, the data dictionary for the different database files. A week later, she subcontracted the programming job to Jay Nunn, an experienced programmer with whom SBIS had a long working relationship.

As always, SBIS told Jay which programming tools and languages to use. This time Odessa instructed him to use 4GO, a fourth generation language and a database management system. Since Odessa considered Plastico's new system small, she figured Jay could finish the job sooner with 4GO than with other more complex application generators. Indeed, 4GO was inflexible, but it had its own advantages: it was efficient, easy to use, and, she believed, sufficiently good for a system of this size.

Odessa gave Jay a free hand. She left it up to him to occasionally meet with Plastico's personnel to assure compliance with their requirements. Two weeks after he started programming, Jay met with Plastico's accountant. The discussion started with the layout of a certain screen and two menus, but it soon proceeded to more general points. Matter-of-factly, the accountant mentioned that she expected the new system to accommodate hundreds of employee records.

"But don't you have just 70 employees?" said Jay.

"Sixty-four, to be exact. But we anticipate growth in the future. This is one of the reasons we are going for this new system. Will there be a problem adding records?"

Jay expected the system to work fine with up to about 200 employee records. But with 400 or 500, with all the bonus and tax calculations, the system might be slow. However, he felt he was not in a position to tell that to the accountant.

"Well, no." Jay started to suspect there was some misunderstanding between Odessa and Plastico. Further discussion revealed that Plastico intended to change its bonus schemes from time to time. The company also needed at least two extra columns in the employee records for attributes not yet recorded about the workers. And they may need more columns in the future, like type and years of education.

Like the other programmers working for SBIS, Jay did most of the work at his home, on his own personal computer. As soon as he was back home, he called Odessa and told her about the discussion with Plastico's accountant. He raised doubts about the suitability of the system for Plastico's needs a year or two into the future. Odessa explained that it was not his business to get into these matters. She was polite but emphatic. Jay tried to convince her to at least talk to Plastico again about their needs.

"Look, Jay," Odessa said, "I was there. I spoke to them. They told me what they needed, and I'm giving them the best they can get for the money. They didn't mention what you just told me."

"Maybe," Jay said, "but my impression is they didn't quite understand everything. Why won't you just tell them there might be some misunderstanding?"

"I'd rather deliver to them exactly what they asked me to. If they want modifications in the future, they can always come back to us. We will gladly serve them."

Jay knew what that meant. If Plastico asked for the modifications after the system was fully developed, the modifications would take more time, and SBIS's profit would be greater. He decided to end the conversation. Odessa wouldn't accept his suggestion anyway.

Jay pressed on and finished the programming within the allotted time, but all that time felt uneasy about the situation.

DISCUSSION QUESTIONS

1. Was it Odessa's responsibility to ask Jeff and his accountant about future needs? Why?
2. Was Odessa's behavior unethical? Why?
3. What would you do if you were Jay? Why?

ETHICS CASE 10

Ethics in Higher Education

Last year Shawn Egan graduated from the University of Michigan with majors in History and English and an excellent 3.8 grade point average. He came from a blue collar family, yet his parents were determined to make every effort to send their three children to the best schools they could get into. Shawn fulfilled his parents' expectations. He applied to the best law schools in the country. Of those that accepted him, he chose Gale University. A few weeks ago, he started his first year as a law student at the prestigious school.

Shawn knew the financial difficulties his family went through to put him through college. He obtained his first degree from a public university; the financial burden was relatively light. But this is Gale, a private school, and like most law students he did not receive any financial aid. He therefore looked for a job as soon as he settled on campus. He wanted to do everything he could to help pay his tuition. A week later, he started work as a clerk for a small law firm in New Maven.

He had to run errands for the firm, make photocopies, and occasionally type documents. The job did not pay much, but he was happy. He wanted to be among lawyers and absorb both the knowledge and the atmosphere. His dream was to eventually open his own law firm, and he felt this was a good, practical, environment in which to learn how to run such an enterprise.

As a law student, Shawn was granted access to the school's computer system. All law students also received a special access code for the LawBase database. The database contains laws, court decisions, and legal literature. It was put together and has been maintained by LawBase, Inc. The company sells permission to use the database to universities and law firms. The renter pays a monthly fee for usage. Once a month the company sends the renter a video disk containing updates: new acts, new court decisions, and abstracts of new legal articles.

Because the service is expensive, only higher education institutions and large law firms subscribe. The small firms usually cannot afford it. They have to look for legal literature using paper indexes and books.

Shawn had good relationships with all the lawyers in the office. All four of them, including Mr. Huchison, were nice to him. But he developed a closer relationship with the youngest of them, Tom Rigley. Tom graduated from law school only two years ago. He often took Shawn to lunch, and usually insisted on paying for it. He was ambitious and worked many hours, sometimes as many as eighty per week.

In a casual conversation over a light lunch, Tom told Shawn how arduous it was to search for verdicts. Court decisions served as precedents for many cases he handled. He complained he had to devote too much time looking for old court decisions and articles interpreting them.

"Oh, if I only had access to one of those databases I used to work with in school," he sighed, leaning back, putting his coffee cup on the table.

"You mean something like LawBase?"

"Oh, yes. We didn't have LawBase, but I hear it's the best."

Shawn opened his mouth to say something, but halted.

"What?" Tom said.

"Well," Shawn said hesitantly, "I have access to LawBase. I don't use it much. I guess I could let you use my computer account."

"Are you sure?" Tom's eyes glittered.

"Why not? I pay for it with my tuition. I use it very little. If it can help you, why not?"

Shawn gave Tom the telephone number through which to connect to Gale's law school computer. He also gave him his own password. Yes, he remembered the policy document he signed at the university. It forbade students and faculty from giving their passwords to other people. But the university pays for the LawBase service anyway, so there is nothing inherently wrong here, he thought.

DISCUSSION QUESTIONS

1. Was Shawn's act unethical? Why or why not?
2. Was Tom's behavior unethical? Why or why not?
3. Briefly discuss the role of higher education institutions in fostering ethical use of information technology.

Ethics in Politics

Dave Williams is an independent systems consultant. Over the ten years since he received his joint degree in computer science and management information systems, he has built himself an excellent reputation. Although he did not have a large operation behind him, his services were purchased by large companies and even governments.

Three years ago, he was invited by the government of Baranda, a small African country, to build its first automated information system. A new department was organized by the country's prime minister, Mr. Ugaba. Mr. Ugaba wanted to modernize Baranda. A close advisor of his suggested that he start by automating data collection and maintenance which could later be analyzed into useful information. The information would be used for planning in agriculture, industry, and education.

Dave spent three months in Baranda. He wrote a long report for Mr. Ugaba. The report detailed his view of an initial system that could gradually be augmented and include all government departments. It also recommended hardware: a mainframe, a few microcomputers, and communications devices. The minister of finance approved the purchase of the equipment, and Dave served as the government's representative in negotiations with vendors.

He returned to America for a short while to purchase software for developing the basic programs. A few weeks after he returned to Baranda, the first skeleton database was in place in the Ministry of Education. Its purpose was to keep records of teachers. Due to the small size of the country, the Minister of Education wanted all the teachers' records in one place. The database was connected to a payroll system that Dave developed. This was the most urgent project, the prime minister told him. Dave quickly trained a few clerks to enter the data, and the database was soon complete. Then Dave moved on to develop systems for the Ministry of Agriculture and the Ministry of Industry.

Dave liked the people of Baranda. He was impressed with their industriousness and their desire to learn. Although the contract he signed with the government rewarded him handsomely for his efforts, he felt it would be unfair to keep his work a secret. He offered Mr. Ugaba the opportunity to assign three to five trainees who would work with him on the remaining systems. This way the country would gain a nucleus of systems developers who could train others. They would also be able to perform some software maintenance duties. Dave realized the knowledge that these people would gain from his on-the-job training would be limited, but it would be better than nothing.

The prime minister accepted his offer enthusiastically. Four young men and a young woman who graduated from liberal art schools in Europe joined him to follow his work. They were eager to learn, and soon became his best friends. When the systems for the two ministries were in place, Dave felt there was a team that could run them reasonably well. He expressed his willingness to always come back and help out if his expertise was required.

Ostensibly, Baranda was a democracy. Elections were held every five years. There were three political parties: The Congress Party, which had won every election so far, and whose leader was the prime minister, Mr. Ugaba; Socialism for Baranda (SB), the main opposition party; and The Liberal Party, a small movement that drew its electorate from the small intelligentsia. In essence, however, Mr. Ugaba and his ministers would not allow any other political power to form a government. They openly bribed voters. They saw to it that ballots from districts known to be sympathetic to the other two parties disappeared before votes were counted. And they sent the police to interfere in conferences and rallies organized by their political opponents, using official allegations of public disorder.

About a month ago, a high official from the Ministry of Education called Dave at his home. He said the Ministry wanted some modifications in the database he built. When asked why his five ex-trainees were not approached, the official said they had been, but they couldn't cope with the technical difficulties. Dave was assured he would be paid handsomely, as in the past. Despite his busy schedule, he remembered his solemn obligation and agreed to help.

As soon as he set foot in Baranda, he felt the atmosphere was different than that of three years ago. He noticed there were significantly more armed soldiers in the airport. People's faces looked tense. The official with whom he had talked on the phone welcomed him, and led him to a limousine. He was rushed to a luxurious hotel. His appointment with the Minister of Education was scheduled for the next morning.

The minister welcomed him warmly and introduced him to a man in his early thirties. The man was Robert Nuwaga, the new head of the agency for government information, the minister said. The minister let Nuwaga explain his needs. In addition to modifications in the Ministry's teachers database, he wanted to establish a network of terminals in the country's schools. The terminals would assist in updating the database.

After the meeting, Dave was driven back to his hotel. He felt at least some of the work could be done by two of his ex-trainees. Why weren't they approached by the minister, he wondered. He pulled a business card from his wallet. On its back there were five handwritten telephone numbers. He called the first one. There was no answer. When he called the next three numbers, a recording said the phones had been disconnected. He then called the fifth number and Emilia, his female trainee, was on the line. She was happy to hear from him but Dave noticed the strain in her voice. They met an hour later in a small restaurant.

Dave noticed a wedding band on her finger. She told him about her husband and one-year-old son. He then asked her about the other four trainees.

"They are all in prison now," she said.

"In prison? Why?"

She explained that since he had left, the power of the socialists grew significantly. The secret police started administrative arrests. Many of the socialist party leaders were imprisoned under the false claim that they had tried to overthrow the government.

Dave told her why he came to Baranda. He described the meeting with the minister and Robert Nuwaga. He noticed a strange expression on her face when he mentioned Nuwaga's name. She told him Nuwaga was the deputy chief of the secret police. The database system Dave had developed, she said, was now used for an additional purpose: monitoring people whom the government suspected were not "loyal."

"How do you know that?" Dave asked.

"I know. I'm not proud of what I'm doing, but I have to. I'm married and have a child. Nuwaga threatened to hurt my family if I refused to collaborate."

Dave had a clearer picture now. The four other trainees did not collaborate and Emilia's knowledge of the system was limited. Therefore, the government called upon him.

He told Robert Nuwaga he would take the job. Nuwaga was generous and offered to pay in advance. Dave said he would rather be paid when the job was done, and the modifications successfully tested, and he and Nuwaga signed the contract. He told Nuwaga that he could not use Emilia for the work.

"If she participates, the job will take longer," he said. "I need no help. I'll do the entire job myself."

That evening he called Baranda Airlines and reserved a seat on a flight back home, scheduled for two days later. The next day he started work. No, he had no intention of fulfilling his part of the contract. He wrote 83 lines of code, a "time bomb." He installed the code in one of the database application programs. The code would destroy the entire database 72 hours later. Two days later he secretly left the country.

Months later he told the story to a colleague. The colleague disagreed with him.

"It's not our duty to pass judgment. If the socialists come to power in that country, they will most probably use the same tactics. Besides, you knowingly signed a contract you did not mean to fulfill. Worse, you maliciously destroyed a system that did not belong to you."

"But what would you do? You don't think these thugs are right, do you?"

"No," his friend said, "I certainly do not. I would simply refuse to do the job."

DISCUSSION QUESTIONS

1. Was Dave's act ethical? Why or why not?
2. Comment on the friend's approach.

Invasion of Privacy

Ace Software Co. is comprised of 14 computer specialists. It specializes in two areas: databases, and digitized graphics and music. Jake and Jonathan Fiedler, the two brothers who started the business, saw a great opportunity in integrating digitized graphics and music into databases. One of the projects they like to boast about is a music education package that they developed for the high school district of their home town.

Despite its small size, Ace gained a very good reputation in the five years of its operation. The Fiedlers selected their employees carefully. They operate their business like a family, and pay bonuses commensurate with performance. The greater the profit on a certain project, the higher the bonus the project team members receive. The employees are professionals who do their work not just for the money, but also out of self-interest and the desire to learn new techniques. The Fiedlers have never rejected a job because of the technical challenge it poses. In two cases they did refuse to accept a job, but the reason was a full schedule.

Last week they signed a contract to develop a sophisticated data collection system for Qmart, a national retail chain. This was the breakthrough the Fiedlers were waiting for. A successful system developed for a large, nationally known company would give their company a great marketing boost. The brothers flew to Farmington Hills, Michigan, to meet with Clinton Davis, Qmart's vice president of information systems.

Clinton introduced himself and his assistant, Linda Yorba. He asked that the content of all their discussions be kept secret. The brothers gave their word. He moved on to describe what Qmart wanted. It was a monitoring and surveillance system. The system's purpose was to collect data from credit cards. That in itself has been done for years by many retailers. Clinton wanted the system to also keep track of the customer's purchases over a period of one year. The brothers suspected some retailers had already implemented such a feature. But here there was an addition: every customer paying with a credit card would be photographed by a hidden camera. The picture would be digitized and kept in the customer record. If the customer paid again with the same card after a period of six months, another picture would be taken and digitized into his or her record. Jonathan asked why the retailer needed the pictures. Clinton said this would give the company a great marketing advantage but he refused to elaborate.

The Fiedlers did not anticipate any technical problems. They asked about Qmart's computing hardware to see if a greater data storage capacity was needed. Digitized pictures took great amounts of storage space. Clinton said he realized the company needed to purchase ROM disks and the appropriate equipment to record and read the collected data. He asked the Fiedlers to evaluate what hardware was needed for the 3,402 stores. He noted that the system should be tested in three or four sites before installing it throughout the chain. Of course, he expected the brothers and their personnel to meet regularly with him and his staff. "I am a great delegator," he said, "and I count one hundred percent on Linda to be our liaison for the project. Don't hesitate to contact her whenever you need help."

The Fiedlers went back home. They met with Clinton and Linda again a week later and a contract was signed. The secrecy clause required strict confidentiality from Ace and its employees. It required that the employees sign a special confidentiality agreement with Ace in which they undertook to keep their work on the project secret not only for the duration of their employment, but also after they leave Ace. The installation of the system in the first site was scheduled for nine months later.

A day later, in their office, the Fiedlers summoned four of their employees. Among them was Nigel MacDonald, the firm's last addition. Nigel came to the U.S. five years ago from England, where he accumulated much experience in digitized graphics and music. He also had a short stint with a company that developed virtual reality games. He was a member of the team that developed the music education system for the high school district. His excellent job there earned him much respect among his colleagues.

When Jonathan described the system they had to build, Nigel was happy. This is the kind of challenge he liked. Jonathan nominated himself project manager. For internal reference, the group named the system Smile, for "Smile, you're on candid camera." The four were asked to finish what they could finish on their current projects, and, in an orderly manner, pass to other employees bigger chunks of work to be completed. Nine months was not a lot of time for this project, and Jonathan wanted to start work immediately. The team met for the first work session two days later.

The project proceeded very well. Nigel and his team members bought two advanced video cameras and other sophisticated gadgets. They tried to minimize the space occupied by the stored data and pictures. They reached a level of sophistication they believed could not be surpassed with the current technology. They felt they were doing a great job.

Usually, Nigel did not discuss work with his wife. But this project really thrilled him, and he felt he must share his experience with someone and who better than Daphne, "my smart and sensitive friend?" He told her he couldn't divulge the name of the client, and made her promise she would not tell anyone about this project. She was a history teacher and had no affinity for computers at all, but she kept asking questions. She finally got to the purpose of the system.

"What do you mean 'what are they going to do with the system'?" he said. "They are going to take customers' pictures and keep them in a database."

"But what do they need customer pictures for?"

"Frankly, my dear, I don't give a damn," he said, mocking Clark Gable in *Gone with the Wind.*

"Well, I'm not sure I wouldn't give a damn."

Nigel's face lost its amused look.

"What do you mean?"

She explained. The next day in the office, he could not concentrate. He kept thinking about their conversation and he finally asked to see Jonathan. He told Jonathan he was "a little concerned" about how the system would be used.

"Nigel, my dear friend, why ask questions? We've got a technically challenging and financially rewarding task. Let's stick to our work."

"Jonathan," Nigel said (they all called each other by their first names), "this system may be used to severely violate people's privacy. The cameras will be hidden, right? Why? I wouldn't want my picture taken without my knowledge."

"Anyone can do that anytime, and there is nothing you can do about it. You call that 'violation of privacy'?"

"Jonathan, it's not only the picture. Qmart uses one of the best satellite communications systems. They can transmit a customer's record from one store to another within seconds, along with shopping habits, credit history, the picture, and whatever else. The communications system allows them to follow individuals throughout their lives, as long as they periodically shop Qmart stores. It may . . ."

"Nigel, relax. I'm sorry, go ahead." Jonathan had never seen the young man so disturbed.

"It may be my British sensitivity to a person's privacy. I don't know. It seems to me there is a great potential here for unjustified invasion of privacy."

"Well, what do you suggest we do?"

"Let's ask them what they will do with the collected data."

"Oh, no, Nigel. We can't do that. We are developing a legitimate information system for a legitimate business. There is nothing illegal in operating a system like this, is there?"

"No, I guess there isn't. But there are many things that are legal and yet immoral."

"Nigel, look," Jonathan tried to calm him down, "we were waiting a long time for a customer like this. Jake and I counted on your experience and enthusiasm when we negotiated this contract. You know you are the most important member of the team. Please calm down. This is a serious corporation, not some back alley peddler. They know what they are doing."

"I—well, never mind."

Jonathan did not say a thing. He just looked at him and shook his head. Nigel felt there was no point in continuing this conversation. He was disturbed. He really liked this project. No. He *loved* it. And he knew Ace had little chance of completing it on time without his participation. But he wanted to be sure the fruits of his efforts were not misused. And he suspected this system would be. It would help invade the privacy of unsuspecting customers. And there are no assurances that an unscrupulous executive would not abuse it for criminal purposes. On the other hand, he pondered, can we blame a gun manufacturer for a crime that was committed with the gun he made?

Back in his office he decided to discuss the matter further with his wife. Perhaps she could resolve his dilemma.

DISCUSSION QUESTIONS

1. Should information technology professionals be concerned about the potential use of their products and services?
2. You are Nigel's wife. What do you suggest he do?

Fraud and Money Theft

Bernice Greenwald had a fifteen year tenure as an EDP (electronic data processing) auditor for First Troy Bank. She had a team of five auditors who performed their jobs at the main office and the eleven branches of the small bank. She reported to the internal auditor, Mr. Chekem. Mr. Chekem had great confidence in Bernice. Although he did not know much about computer-based information systems beyond the use of electronic spreadsheets and word processors, he acknowledged their importance in banking. Therefore, he gave Bernice a free hand to send the auditors to many professional meetings and continued education courses in the field.

Bernice had a weekly meeting with her small crew every Friday morning. In the meeting, she laid out the plans for their audit work for the following week. Much of the work was routine. However, it was important to conduct surprise checks in the branches. The purpose of this activity was twofold. First, it gave the tellers and other employees a sense that their work was under scrutiny. Second, it was necessary to catch fraud when the culprit was unsuspecting.

During her tenure, Bernice personally discovered three fraud cases that involved the abuse of computers. The last case occurred four years ago. She used to jest about this long "clean" period of time: "Who knows why we don't find any fraud cases? We're either doing an excellent job, or a lousy job." Deep in her heart, she yearned to discover a fraud case. As in the past, she would probably be summoned by the bank's president, be congratulated on a job well done, and be granted a bonus check.

Last January she went with one of her auditors to conduct a routine check in one of the branches. They planned to spend the entire afternoon there. As always, they asked for computer reports and examined them carefully. They also looked into some of the on-line systems. Through her work for the bank, Bernice knew not only the output of the programs, but also the programs themselves. She had access to the source and object codes. This was important in case someone changed a program with the intention to commit fraud.

This time something caught her attention. She found a series of new accounts with balances of exactly $25, the minimum required of a customer to open an account. There was also one new account, with a balance of $1,000,024. The last transaction in this account took place the previous day. It was a transfer of $999,999. Such figures always alerted Bernice and her auditors. Any wire transfer of less than $1 million could be authorized by a single officer, with the rank of deputy branch manager or up. The history of wire fraud shows that criminals are careful not to exceed such limits if they are aware of the less stringent security measures for the lower sums.

She asked the branch manager for details of the individuals who opened the new accounts. The names and addresses varied. She examined the file of the account with the suspected balance, which was a small company. She then asked for all the documents of the company's transactions for the past months. The longer she examined the documents, the more suspicious she was that something was wrong.

Bernice asked the branch manager not to discuss her audit with anyone. Since she suspected something fishy, she wanted the branch employees to continue with their regular activities, and if someone was doing something against bank policy, that person would not suspect anything. Her monitoring of the small company's transactions went on. She was looking especially for intra-bank fund transfers.

After three weeks, her suspicion was confirmed. There was an increasing number of fund transfers from other accounts into the company's account. Bernice's investigation showed that the transfers did not come from accounts owned by customers of the company and that the balance was now over $7 million. She asked the branch manager to telephone her as soon as a large amount was withdrawn from the account. It was like an ambush.

Finally it happened. A sum of $6 million was withdrawn and transferred to accounts in five different banks in New York. The branch manager called Bernice and she immediately gathered information about the transactions. Apparently, an officer at the bank's headquarters gave the order for the transfers.

Bernice's investigation revealed a fraud scheme. The officer, Milton Burns, was a twenty-year veteran of the bank. He abused his signature authorization to transfer funds from "dormant" accounts to the company's account. "Dormant" accounts are those that are inactive for long periods of time. It was easy for the officer to find and keep track of these accounts through a small computer program that he had asked a programmer to write for him and install on the computer in his office.

Bernice met with the bank's president, Mr. Trickle. She gave him the findings of her investigation. There was no doubt in her mind the bank would press criminal, and maybe civil, charges. This was grand-scale fraud. She also received Mr. Trickle's authorization to contact the other banks and try to freeze the stolen money. In four of the five banks, the money had been withdrawn before she called. In the fifth bank, only $320,000 was left of the original deposit of $950,000. Bernice reported the facts to Mr. Trickle.

For three weeks nothing happened. When Bernice asked about Burns, she was told by the secretary that "Mr. Burns is on vacation." Bernice was sure he had been suspended until charges were pressed. She asked to meet with the president again. This time, the bank's counsel, Jerry Law, was present at the meeting.

"What's going on with Burns? Aren't you going to press charges?"

"No, Bernice. And Jerry will explain why."

Jerry leaned forward.

"Burns agreed to return $320,000 to the bank. He had more than one collaborator and he doesn't know where the rest of the money is. It would take a long time for the district attorney to collect evidence against all the collaborators."

"But look at the message we are sending." Bernice turned to Mr. Trickle, trying to invoke *his* reaction. She never liked Jerry, nor did she like his reasoning.

Trickle kept silent and Jerry responded for him.

"We are not sending any message, Bernice. We don't want to send any messages. We want to put a lid on the whole thing and forget it. The damage that the publicity would cause is far greater than what we could gain. This is not a vendetta. This is pure business."

"And what are you going to do to Burns? You are not letting him go on with his career as if nothing happened, are you?"

"No. He agreed to retire without severance pay."

Bernice felt that she was going to explode.

"Without severance pay, huh? He doesn't need any severance pay now!"

"Bernice, please," Mr. Trickle tried to calm her down. "You did a good job. If it weren't for you, the scam would most probably go on, and the damage would be greater. We appreciate what you have done for the bank, but we have to consider the overall picture. This is strictly business."

Bernice left the meeting frustrated. Something was wrong here. Very wrong.

DISCUSSION QUESTIONS

1. What would you do if you were Bernice? Why?
2. Would you act differently than Mr. Trickle did? Why or why not?

First Amendment Rights

Oliver Chong is an enthusiastic computer user. He started playing with computers when he was nine years old. Now he is a student at Barmouth College. Barmouth is a prestigious, high-tuition school located in New England. His parents were glad when he was accepted to the school. The high tuition did not concern them. Oliver's father is a successful lawyer. Money has never been a problem for the Chongs.

Oliver is a journalism major. Although he is only a freshman, he has managed to become a member of the editing board of *Trumpet,* the student newspaper. Fact is, he is the only freshman on the board. He convinced the other members of the board that his services were needed due to his experience with word processing and desktop publishing. He also befriended four of the seven members. When one of them graduated and left campus, Oliver realized his little dream.

Indeed, he proved that his participation in the board's work was valuable. His initiative yielded a revamped humor column and the Faculty on Fire column. For the latter, he interviewed a faculty member every week. His questions were provocative. The students liked his contribution.

Three months ago Oliver convinced the editorial board to start a computerized spinoff of *Trumpet.* He wanted to replicate *Trumpet* on a bulletin board system (BBS), so that students could access it through their computers as long as they had modems. He hoped students from other New England universities would also connect to it, contribute ideas, and participate in a large medium of communication.

The student council did not approve the funds for the BBS. The majority of the council members felt that the printed newspaper satisfied the needs of the student community. An appeal to the Dean of Student Affairs received the same response. As Oliver was adamant on establishing the BBS, he decided to volunteer his own computer. He had an IBM compatible computer with 80 MB of hard disk memory. He figured he could start the BBS with that amount of memory, and if it succeeded, he would turn to the student council again to fund the extra memory devices.

The BBS was an immediate success. Initially, Oliver and Arch, his roommate in the dorms, put only the *Trumpet* issues on it. Soon they invited the students to post E-mail personal messages and "swap and shop" ads. Oliver and his friend named the bulletin board *BBS Trumpet.* Additional columns opened. Students contributed jokes, stories, and poems. They critiqued professors. They put on invitations for parties. Oliver was happy.

Word reached the corporations in and around town about *BBS Trumpet.* A law firm approached Oliver and asked to place an ad for student assistants for its office. Oliver and Arch considered it, and decided to allow commercial ads for a fee. They agreed to turn in all the fees collected to the student council, if the council approved the purchase of additional equipment. The council agreed. After the first help wanted ad, more corporations placed their own ads.

But one bright morning two stern-looking men came to meet with the Dean of Student Affairs. When they left the office, they headed straight to the men's dorms. They knocked on the door to Oliver's and Arch's room. Arch opened the door. They presented a court warrant.

"We are with the Secret Service," the shorter man said. "We have a warrant to search the premises."

"What is this? What are you looking for?" Arch tried to stand in the men's way, but they stepped forward.

"I think we found what we wanted," said the taller man. He was looking at the computer standing on the table. "Please unplug the PC and all the peripheral equipment, sir."

"Hold it, just . . . hold it." Arch positioned himself between the table and the men. "Will you please tell me what's going on?"

"Okay," said the shorter man, who seemed to be the other's superior.

He explained. Four weeks ago the database of a large bank was penetrated. Whoever accessed the computer system left rude messages on the system. The system was penetrated five more times and each time the intruder left ruder and ruder messages. In the last intrusion some twenty customer accounts were messed up. This time the hacker left details that led to Barmouth College. A massive investigation revealed that the last access was made from Oliver's and Arch's telephone line. It was the telephone line dedicated to *BBS Trumpet.*

Arch knew he was not the culprit, but he could not believe Oliver would do such a thing. The men unplugged the computer, the modem, and the disk drives. They took the devices and put them in their car. They then came back to the room and searched it.

"Bingo!" said the tall man. He held a notebook sheet in his right hand.

"Access codes?" asked the other man.

"Just one. But that's good enough."

Arch was stunned. The men pulled the sheet from Oliver's desk drawer. As soon as the men left, he looked up Oliver's class schedule. He ran to the classroom, opened the door, and, much to the professor's surprise, called Oliver. They returned to the dorms where Oliver admitted to having accessed the bank's database.

"These guys are crazy," he said, "it was just a prank. They can't take my computer!"

"Well, they did. They had a court warrant. I suggest you call your father. Now."

Oliver called his father. Mr. Chong took the first available flight, rented a car, and drove to the campus. He admonished his son for his wrong deed, but disagreed with the confiscation. As word reached the other users, students and corporations, they all expressed their anger. Arch wrote up an official protest letter. He collected signatures from students, and many of the corporations that used the BBS authorized their officers to add their signatures. The letter was published in *Trumpet* and was sent to other newspapers in town. A copy was sent to the head of the Secret Service in Washington, D.C.

The letter read:

We, the users of *BBS Trumpet,* students, corporations, and private citizens, protest the confiscation of the computer and other hardware which served the electronic bulletin board. Regardless of whether the owner of the equipment committed a crime or not, *BBS Trumpet* served as an important means of communication. It would be inconceivable to confiscate a radio station or a newspaper press because a crime was allegedly committed through their use. An electronic bulletin board is no different. The first amendment to the U.S. Constitution protects our right to free speech and freedom of the press. The confiscation by the Secret Service was a blatant violation of this right. We demand that the equipment be returned immediately.

DISCUSSION QUESTIONS

1. Do you agree with the letter? Why or why not?
2. The letter demands the return of the confiscated equipment. If the hardware is returned, should Oliver be allowed to use it:
   a. until he is convicted or acquitted in court?
   b. after he is convicted (if he is not imprisoned)?
3. In this case, the computer belonged to Oliver. Suppose the computer belonged to the university. Would you justify the confiscation?

Obligations to Society

In his fourteen years at BBM (Bolz Beranech Marconi), Alex Franco acquired much experience in the artificial intelligence (AI) field. He was a member of the first team that developed an expert system for the military. When that project ended successfully, he joined a team that developed a natural language processing program. He later participated in the development of two artificial vision systems. You might say that except for pure robotics, he had experience in every aspect of AI.

BBM worked mainly for the U.S. Navy. Over the years, Alex befriended many of the Navy engineers who worked in the Department of the Navy in Washington, D.C. They had great respect for his professionalism. Two years ago, he amicably left BBM to work as a private consultant. The Navy hired his services to develop a new system for its aircraft. The computer-based system was to identify friend or foe according to visual data.

Every military force has a serious problem: how to identify military objects when radio communication fails or is impossible. Identification is especially difficult at night and in inclement weather. Misidentification is the main reason for fratricide, killing your fellow soldiers, or as it is known in the public, casualties by "friendly fire."

The Navy wanted a better identification system, one that would take into consideration details like formation of vehicles and vessels, and silhouettes of vehicles and vessels from every possible angle. One innovative detail was a special paint: When a laser beam hit the substance it reflected invisible light that could be recognized by a special sensor. The sensor was to be connected to the ID system and, along with the other details, give a percentage probability. The probability (e.g., 45 percent or 98 percent) indicated to the pilot the chances that the target was an enemy vehicle or vessel.

Alex was excited to participate in this top secret project. Rear Admiral Daryl Robins, who headed the project, told him several times that the Navy counted on him to develop the best system feasible. Of course, the system did not consist only of his AI software, but his computer programs were its "brain."

After seventeen months, the initial version of the system was ready. The Navy conducted simulations of combat situations. The success rate was high. The brass were happy. So were the civilians involved, among them Alex. He took another month to improve details that were unsatisfactory in the simulations. In the second simulation series, the results were better. Although the project was two months behind schedule, Daryl praised the men and women for doing an excellent job.

Then the "wet" test started. Real vehicles, tanks, troop carriers, and helicopters were assigned as potential targets. Some were brought to the test field from the battlefields of Kuwait and southern Iraq. This time the results were not as good. Daryl was not discouraged. Nor did he blame anyone for the not-so-glamorous results.

Alex asked everyone to try and analyze the results so that they could converge on the reasons for the discrepancies between the performance in the simulation and the "wet" test. Every other day, the team met with Dayrl and reported their findings. Lessons were learned and another "wet" test was scheduled. The results were not better. On the average, an enemy vehicle was identified with a 90 percent probability 76 percent of the time. Friendly vehicles were identified with a 90 percent probability only 63 percent of the time. The 90 percent probability was a dictated standard.

Alex asked the Navy officers on the team to try and think of additional "variables." What they called "attributes," that is, shapes, colors, the manner in which a vehicle moved, etc., he called variables. The point was not the semantics, of course. The more attributes he could use in the computer program, the better the chances of accurate identification. The officers conducted debriefings with their colleagues from the aircraft carriers and the Air Force. They received more attributes. Bill updated the ID system. The third test raised the average results to 82 percent enemy vehicles and 76 percent friendly vehicles for the 90 percent probability, but Alex was not happy. The officers told him they had no more attributes to contribute. He asked to see Daryl.

Daryl welcomed him into his office.

"Alex, my good friend, have a seat. What can I do for you?"

"Well, I wanted to tell you that I will not be able to improve the system's ID capabilities in the near future. That is, if the Navy accepts the system for installation, it accepts it as is." He paused to see Daryl's reaction.

"So?"

"So the percentages will not be higher until the next update. And the next update can come from data collected from real action."

"So?" Daryl did not seem to get the point.

"Are you satisfied with the last test's results?"

"I'm not thrilled, but they satisfy me. Why do you ask?"

Alex moved uneasily in his chair. Daryl leaned forward and asked in a fatherly tone:

"Alex, what's bothering you? You have done a good job. You didn't expect a pat on the back from me, did you? You know I appreciate your work."

"No, I'm not expecting a pat on the back. I'm concerned about something else. I understand the system is scheduled to be installed in the Navy and Air Force as scheduled, in July."

Daryl's face turned tense now.

"Affirmative."

"I'm afraid the system is not good enough to be installed in those aircraft."

Daryl wanted to say "who the hell are you to tell us what to do with our aircraft?" But he contained his emotions. He had great respect for Alex and did not want to offend him.

"This system is better than any ID system we have ever had, right?"

"Right. However, I understand the pilots and navigators will not be aware of the success rates we achieved in the field tests."

"So? They still get the best system they've ever had."

"Why won't you tell them about the system's limitations?"

"Alex, with all due respect, that is up to us to decide. We know how soldiers behave in the battlefield. It is best that the pilots use the tools they are given. They have to react to difficult situations within seconds. We can't confuse them with success rates."

"But I'm afraid they will overrely on it. They will not be aware of its limitations."

Daryl was becoming impatient now.

"Alex, can you improve the rates?"

"No. Not until I receive more attributes."

"Well, then we will install the system as is. Is there anything else you wanted to talk to me about?"

"No, sir. Thank you for your time."

Alex left. For two days he could not concentrate. He firmly believed that the Navy should either dig deeper to find more attributes that would allow him to improve his computer program, or disclose the system's current success rates. What could he do? He could blow the whistle, but that would be a clear violation of the confidentiality agreement he had signed. Or he could keep quiet and enjoy the military's compliment on a job well done.

That night he had an awful dream. He was sitting in a fighter's cockpit, hunting for enemy vehicles. It was a dark night with very little moonlight. The ID system he helped develop indicated he was approaching enemy vehicles. He readied his missile launchers. He asked for information from the ground. The officer said no friendly vehicles were marked on his map in that area. Alex looked again at the system's screen. The vehicles' silhouettes did not look familiar. He fired a missile. There was silence in the radio. Then he heard the ground officer saying calmly: "Congratulations. You just shot one of our troop carriers." He woke up in a cold sweat.

DISCUSSION QUESTIONS

1. You are Alex. What will you do?
2. What are the circumstances under which an IT (information technology) professional should violate a contract with a client? Explain.

Confidentiality

Jennie Cheng opened the envelope she just received in the mail. She pulled the document out, took a quick look at it, and smiled. "Great. Here's work." The letter was from F&F, a small retail chain in Chicago. It invited her to send in a proposal for the implementation of a new consumer database. This could be her great chance.

Six months earlier Jennie had left United Market Research, Inc. (UMR), a Chicago company that provides market research services. The company collects data from the public, analyzes it, and sells the results of the study to the client who ordered it. It employs statisticians to design the samples and perform the analysis. To collect the data, the company uses part-time workers, mainly students, who call people who fit the sample criteria.

Over the two decades of practice, UMR's managers learned that many people refused to provide personal information. Its own study showed that the main reason was people's fear that the information would later be used to harass them with junk mail, or even be used against them. Therefore, five years ago management decided to adopt a new policy: the surveyors promised the surveyed individuals that the information they provided would not be used on an individual basis, and that it would be destroyed immediately after the statistical analysis. Also, UMR lured respondents with small tokens of appreciation: keychains, cheap digital watches, etc., which were supplied by the companies that ordered the studies.

Jennie worked for UMR as a database specialist. She developed databases and applications that were used to store, retrieve, and manipulate data. She worked closely with the statisticians to accommodate their research needs. She enjoyed her job, but dreamt of starting a business of her own. She stayed at UMR long enough to acquire experience. UMR's management tried to convince her to stay, but her mind was made up. Her superiors did not have hard feelings; on the contrary, she received severance pay and was invited to offer her services to the company as an independent consultant.

But she was never contacted by UMR. She performed little programming jobs for small businesses, and consulted with them on hardware and software. It was a decent living, but not the professional challenge she yearned for. A few weeks ago, she met an old friend who was a store manager for F&F. The friend said the company was going to install a new customer databank for its marketing offensive. He knew very little about it, so Jennie asked him to inquire about the project. He did, and gave Jennie the necessary details. She called the appropriate people at F&F and asked to participate in the bidding.

Jennie immediately sat down to study F&F's requirements. She typed up a price proposal, drawing much pleasure from submitting one on her own letterhead. She mailed the proposal and hoped for the best.

F&F's selection process was short. Less than a month later, Jennie received a letter inviting her to sign a contract with the company. That same day, she called two programmers to help her. A few hours after she signed the contract, she hired them on an ad hoc basis.

Jennie and her programmers worked fast. Jennie laid out the logical design of the database and the three of them considered the software tools that would best fit this project. They selected a fourth generation programming language with which they were familiar and wrote the code. The team built the system in modules. When the first module was ready, Jennie asked F&F managers for copies of real records for testing.

F&F did not collect data. It bought data from data companies and credit card companies. Jennie and her programmers studied the format of the data on the purchased magnetic tapes. One of the programmers wrote a program to read the records from the tape and store them on F&F hard disks. When the data from the first tape was loaded into the database, Jennie tried the completed module.

As she was testing the different features, she felt that some of the data were familiar. She examined more records.

"I have seen these records before. I swear I have," she whispered while the records scrolled on the monitor.

"What d'ya mean you've seen the records?" the programmer asked.

"I'm telling you, Stan, I've seen this before, but I can't remember where."

It was close to 6 p.m. Jennie and the programmers left the F&F facility. On her way, while standing at a red light, she remembered. Of course. She *did* see the information before. When she arrived at her apartment, she called F&F, but the person she wanted to speak with had left. She tried again in the morning and the manager was available. Jennie tried to sound as calm as possible. After exchanging pleasantries, she asked:

"Mr. Ehrlich, can you tell me where you purchased your tapes for the new database?"

"Well, we used several sources. Could you be more specific?"

"Yes. Who sold you the tape you gave me yesterday?"

"If you give me a second, I'll check," Mr. Ehrlich answered. He was the manager that F&F assigned to be the liaison between management and Jennie. After a few seconds he was back on the phone.

"This one came from UMR."

"That's what I thought," Jennie said. "That's what I thought."

"Ms. Cheng, you sound concerned. Is anything wrong?"

"Can I see you in your office now—I mean in about an hour?" Jennie was disturbed. She wanted to clarify this business immediately.

One hour later she met Ehrlich.

"Mr. Ehrlich, the tape you bought from UMR should not have been sold to you."

"What do you mean? Why?"

Jennie explained that UMR had betrayed the people who took part in its surveys. Jennie felt that this was probably not the only tape UMR had sold to other companies. Ehrlich said F&F had not been told by UMR about its obligation to destroy the data.

"We are buying these tapes for good money. I doubt that management would willingly agree to not use them."

"I think you should talk to them," Jennie said.

"No, Ms. Cheng. With all due respect, if you want to talk to them, that's fine with me. But I won't. My job is to help you with your project. I hope this will not hamper our effort to put the system in place in time."

Jennie didn't know what Ehrlich meant by "our effort." She felt like dropping the whole project. She did not want to be a part of this grand-scale deception. Although she could lose money, she was ready to stop work now. But it was not that easy. On the one hand she was bound by contract to finish the project. On the other hand, if she did finish it, F&F would use UMR's tapes. In addition, the problem was not just this particular project. She felt something should be done about UMR's unethical practice. She could contact a newspaper or a television station and blow the whistle on UMR, but the company had been her employer, and she did not want to harm her colleagues still there.

"Why don't I ask AISP?" she thought. "Let's see what they have to say about this." AISP (Association of Information Systems Professionals) was a large professional organization and Jennie had been a member since she graduated from college. All members had to accept AISP's *Code of Ethical Standards*.

Jennie called a member of AISP's Ethics Committee. The lady who answered her call said she was the chairperson of the Ethics Committee. She said she appreciated Jennie's concern, but could not give her any advice. "I know what *I* would do," she said, "but I cannot tell you what to do. If you read the *Code* again, you will see that the decision is the member's alone. It is our policy not to give an opinion or intervene in individual cases. I'm sorry."

DISCUSSION QUESTIONS

1. Do you agree with Ehrlich's behavior? What would you do?
2. Professional organizations of Information Technology practitioners often leave the individual professional to cope with his or her own ethical dilemma. Do you accept this approach? Why? If you don't, what should organizations do to help the individual?
3. You are Jennie. What do you do now?